Write English with Tengwar

A Workbook for English General Use

By Fiona Jallings

©2020 by Fiona Jallings.

All rights reserved, including the right to reproduce this book or portions thereof in any form whatsoever, except for review purposes.

Material from J. R. R. Tolkien's works are represented here with the permission of the Tolkien Estate and may not be reproduced without their prior consent.

ISBN: 9781654355821

Table of Contents

Acknowledgments 2
Introduction 3
Most Effective Use of This Book 4
Fonts 4
Vocabulary 5
Organization of Consonants 5
The Tengwar Chart 6
The Tehtar 7
Numbers 8
Shorthand Words 8
Capital Letters, Underlining, and Red Ink 9
Punctuation Marks 9
Paragraphs 10
Alphabetic Tengwar Quick Reference Sheet 11
Practice Writing 12
    Tyellë 1: Voiceless Stops 12
    Vowel Carriers and Vowel A 12
    Tyellë 2: Voiced Stops and Vowel E 14
    Tyellë 3: Voiceless Fricatives and Vowel I 16
    Extended Voiceless Tengwar and Silent E 18
    Tyellë 4: Voiced Fricatives and Vowel O 20
    Extended Voiced Tengwar 22
    Tyellë 5: Nasals and Vowel U 24
    Tyellë 6: Approximants and Vowel Y 26
    Tyellë 7: More Approximants and Double Vowels AA 28
    Tyellë 8: S and Z and Double Vowels EE 30
    Tyellë 9: H and WH and Double Vowels OO and UU 32
    Digraphs 34
        -A Digraphs and Double Consonants 34
        -E Digraphs and Nasals + Stops 36
        -I/Y Digraphs and the W-Tehta 38
        -U/W Digraphs and the S-Tehta 40
    Christopher's Numbers 42
    Tolkien's Numbers 44
    Shorthand Words 46
    Punctuation Marks 47
        Dots 47
        Sentences 48
        Paragraphs, Verses, and Texts 49
Let's Put it All Together! 50
Answer Key 53

Acknowledgments

The works on which my research for this book has been based, notably those of J R R Tolkien himself and his son Christopher Tolkien, are works protected by copyright throughout the world. Anyone wishing to quote from these works in their own publications must seek their own permission from the Tolkien Estate and any other relevant copyright owner.

In especial, my research draws from the following sources:

The Lord of the Rings by J. R. R. Tolkien.
Sauron Defeated written by J. R. R. Tolkien and edited by Christopher Tolkien.
J. R. R. Tolkien Artist & Illustrator by Wayne G. Hammond and Christina Scull.
The Letters of J. R. R. Tolkien edited by Humphrey Carpenter.
Parma Eldalamberon no. 20 edited by Christopher Gilson and Arden Smith.
Vinyar Tengwar issue 23 edited by Carl F. Hostetter.

Special thanks to Måns Björkman and his extensive scholarly work on Tolkien's writing systems that is available free on his website, *Amanye Tenceli*[1].

Thanks to the font developers who made it possible to type in tengwar:

J. 'Mach' Wust of the *Free Tengwar Font Project*[2].
Johan Winge, maker of *Tengwar Telcontar* and *Tengwar Annatar*.
Dan Smith, maker of *Tengwar Noldor*.

J. R. R. Tolkien's scripts, on which the fonts used in this book are based, are themselves also works protected by copyright throughout the world, and use of them also requires the permission of the Tolkien Estate.

Thanks also to:

My editor, Mark Rosenfelder, who helped me organize this mess.
My copy-editor, Adam Elliott, who found all my errant commas.
My beta readers, who are just awesome.
Edith Wietek who made the pretty cover.
My cat, Muior, who slept on my toes.

---

[1] http://at.mansbjorkman.net/
[2] http://freetengwar.sourceforge.net/

Introduction

Welcome to the wonderful world of tengwar! J.R.R. Tolkien invented them as a writing system for his Noldorin Elves. For this particular script he credited the elf Fëanor. If you have any linguistic training, you'll notice that the tengwar chart looks suspiciously like an IPA chart, because Fëanor was a super special awesome elf who was also a linguist.

Tolkien set up the tengwar to be very flexible and easily adapted to the sounds of any language. Whole columns of tengwar can have their values reassigned to match whatever language they're used with. This means you can't use the system described here for any other language. What's a voiced TH in English is a DH in Sindarin and an NT in Quenya.

There are two different approaches to writing English in tengwar called *modes*: **phonetic** (based on the sounds of the language) and **orthographic** (based on the spellings of the words). The phonetic mode requires some linguistic knowledge, so this booklet focuses on the orthographic mode. This allows us to pretend that we've been using tengwar to write English for a thousand years because the history of the words is reflected in their spellings.

Another set of modes are a **Full Mode**, which uses tengwar to stand for vowels, and an **Ómatehtar Mode**, called **General Use**, which uses marks called *tehtar* over and under the tengwar to stand for vowels and some consonants. People really love the look of the General Use because it's what was used on the One Ring and *The Lord of the Rings* title-page decoration; therefore, this booklet focuses on it.

Even though this version of General Use is based on how we spell words in English, there still is a heavy component of how the words are pronounced that will affect how you write the words. Many distinctions that aren't made when writing with the Latin alphabet are made when writing with tengwar. Tolkien updated and redid his system for orthographic tengwar many, many times, with varying dependence on phonetics, and every expert has their own preferences. I've attempted to find a decent middle-ground that most Tolkien-scholars can agree on.

I write tengwar according to my own accent (Northwestern US). You don't have to conform to my accent to be correct, and I encourage you to think about how you yourself pronounce the words. For example, in my dialect the TH in "with" is voiceless, but for British English speakers, that TH is voiced. A British person would write the title of this workbook differently:

Now that you know what you're getting into, let's start learning!

Most Effective Use of This Book

This book will not be enough to teach you how to use Orthographic General Use Tengwar for English. No single book could. You're going to need a lot of practice to make this stick. I have a couple of suggestions that will help.

To start, make flashcards as you learn the symbols. Drawing the flashcards by hand helps with kinetic learning, and you'll be able to practice recognizing the symbols with the cards you make.

Then, after you have finished the book, practice writing with the script daily. Have a grocery list? Write it with tengwar. A diary? Tolkien wrote his with tengwar too. I sometimes just copy random pages of books with tengwar to keep my skills up. If you want to make this skill stick, daily repetition will help you more than anything else.

Fonts

I'm not going to teach you how to use any tengwar fonts in this book for several reasons.

The first is that I don't need to. Each of the fonts comes with documentation. This documentation covers the key-mapping and how to use it. Sometimes (with the Dan Smith fonts in particular) they include quick reference sheets. Those who ignore this documentation make the error of trying to take texts and put them directly into those fonts without realizing that no tengwar font uses a QWERTY key-map!

Another reason that I'm not covering the fonts is that you need to learn the tengwar first. The key-maps won't help you if you don't already know which symbols you're looking for. Trying to juggle multiple reference charts and the key-maps will make your progress very slow and frustrating. Learning to use a tengwar font means relearning how to type, and it'll go much faster if you already know your tengwar.

Lastly, if you try to do the fonts before you've learned the tengwar, you won't be able to check your work as you write. I've seen a lot of tengwar texts in which whole chunks of sentences or paragraphs are missing because the writer couldn't read what they'd just written.

These three things—ignoring the font's documentation, not being able to read the key-maps, and not being able to check one's work—are responsible for the vast majority of terrible tengwar online. Let's do our best to improve this, shall we?

Vocabulary

First off, here is the word for what this book is teaching you to do.

Transliterate *v.* to take a text and write it with a different writing system without translating it.

Because Tolkien made this script for his Quenya-speaking elves, all of the vocabulary for describing it is in Quenya. Plurals are made with the **-r** suffix.

- **Tengwa** "letter"
- **Telco** "stem" the straight line in a tengwa
- **Lúva** "bow" the curved line in a tengwa
- **Tehta** "mark" diacritics, or accents on the tengwa
- **Téma** "column"
- **Tyellë** "row" (plural **tyeller**)

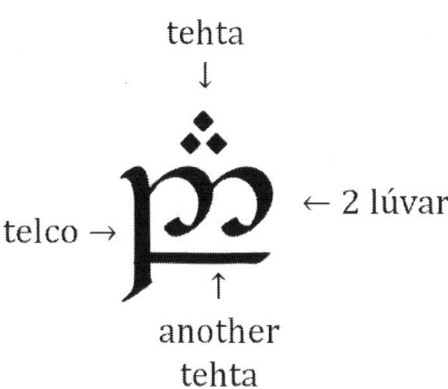

Organization of Consonants

The consonants are organized quite similarly to the way that linguists organize them. The témar are organized by where the sounds are made and are named after the tengwar in the top tyellë.

1. Tincotéma: Alveolar Sounds (made at the ridge behind one's teeth)
2. Parmatéma: Labial Sounds (made at the lips)
3. Calmatéma: Palatal Sounds (made at the palate)
4. Quessetéma: Velar Sounds (made at the back of the mouth)

The first six tyeller are also linguistically organized by how the sounds are made.

1. First tyellë: Voiceless stops (whispered, air stopped then released)
2. Second tyellë: Voiced stops (air stopped then released)
3. Third tyellë: Voiceless fricatives (whispered, air is pressurized into a hiss)
4. Fourth tyellë: Voiced fricatives (air is pressurized into a buzz)
5. Fifth tyellë: Nasals (air is pushed through the nose)
6. Sixth tyellë: Approximants (sounds are really close to being vowels)

Tyeller seven through ten are leftover symbols that don't fit gracefully into the chart.

The tengwar have Quenya names, which are based on the sounds they represent in Quenya. They are all words featuring their Quenya sounds, so they won't match exactly the sounds they represent in English.

Tengwar with black backgrounds aren't used for writing in the English Orthographic General Use.

5

The Tengwar Chart

	Tincotéma	Parmatéma	Calmatéma	Quessetéma
Tyellë 1	Tinco T	Parma P	Calma CH	Quessë C/K
Tyellë 2	Ando D	Umbar B	Anga J	Ungwë G
Tyellë 3	Thúlë TH	Formen F	Harma SH	Hwesta CH
Tyellë 4	Anto TH	Ampa V	Anca ZH	Unquë GH
Tyellë 5	Númen N	Malta M	Ñoldo	Ñwalmë NG
Tyellë 6	Órë R	Vala W	Anna Y	Wilya
Tyellë 7	Rómen R	Arda	Lambë L	Alda
Tyellë 8	Silmë S	Silmë Nuquerna C	Ázë Z	Ázë Nuquerna Z
Tyellë 9	Hyarmen H	Hwesta Sindarinwa WH	Yanta -E	Úrë
Tyellë 10	Halla	Telco vowel carrier	Ára vowel carrier	Ossë -A

The Tehtar

Here are the vowel tehtar. They go on the tengwa following them. The dotted circles mark where the tengwar will go.

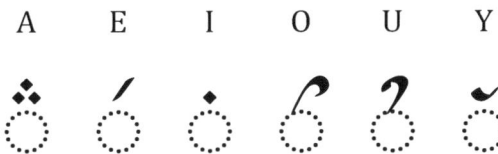

These are consonant tehtar. They go on the tengwa in front of them. The silent E isn't counted as a vowel, and it also goes on the previous tengwa.

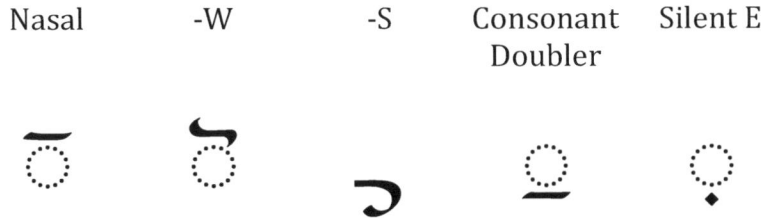

The only consonant tehta that doesn't go on the previous tengwa is the *nasal tehta*, which can only be put on tyeller 1, 2, and 5. It marks an N before the tengwa most of the time, but before the parmatéma, it becomes an M, as in "empath" and "amber."

The order for piling all of these tehtar onto a tengwa is:

The word above would spell "annnwe." You'll never need to pile all of the tehtar onto a tengwa like this, but there will be instances where you'll be piling multiple tehtar on top of each other.

7

Numbers

Tolkien devised at least four number systems for tengwar that we know about. Here are two of them—the one favored by fans and the best attested one.

The first was reported to us by his son Christopher Tolkien, and it's popular with fans because fans learned about it first. It's distinct from the other tengwar.

0	1	2	3	4	5	6	7	8	9

This system is written with the smallest place first and largest place last—the opposite of how we do it with the Arabic numerals. Thus, it's 1's place, then 10's, then 100's, then 1000's, and so on. For example, 2046 would be written 6402:

The second system comes from Tolkien himself. It wasn't published until 2012, so fewer fans know about it. In it, a variety of tengwar stand for numbers.

0	1	2	3	4	5	6	7	8	9

In this system, the numbers are written in the same order as we would put them, with the largest place first and the smallest place last. For example, the number 2046:

Shorthand Words

These are the known abbreviations for common words.

the   of   of the   and

Capital Letters, Underlining, and Red Ink

There aren't capital letters as we tend to think of them in tengwar. A big, fancy tengwa is used for emphasizing important words or names or to mark the beginnings of paragraphs. Just starting a sentence isn't a reason to use one of these, and plenty of texts don't bother with them at all.

Underlining a word or changing the color of the ink from black to red has the same meaning that using a capital letter does: it draws the eye to that word or name to show its importance. Red ink and underlining aren't used on the first word of a paragraph, unless that word is also an important, emphasized one.

These three text flourishes should only be used for fancy, formal documents.

Punctuation Marks

Tolkien was very inconsistent about the punctuation he used. Sometimes he used Latin punctuation, which I don't need to teach you because you already know it. Instead, we'll focus on the non-Latin punctuation systems that he used. When he was doing a non-Latin styled text, Tolkien didn't use anything equivalent to apostrophes or word-joining dashes.

There are several different types of punctuation marks. They get a space on either side of them unless they are at the beginning or end of a line.

Dots stand for pauses. The more dots, the stronger and more end-like the pause.

- · comma/semicolon

- : period

- ∴ period/paragraph ender

- :: paragraph ender

- ⁘ line break/paragraph end

Question marks and exclamation points replace periods at the ends of sentences.

- ʃ exclamation point

- ß question mark

Parentheses have a variety of forms. The short beginning and ending parentheses are also used to mark switching to a different tengwar mode or language.

⁓ or ⁋ parentheses

⁋ starting parenthesis

⁋ ending parenthesis

The double-bar is used to mark a word broken up because it couldn't fit onto a line. It's also perfectly acceptable to just break up words when they don't fit on a line without marking them.

≈ hyphen for words broken up at the end of a line

Paragraphs

There are four ways to distinguish paragraphs from each other.

1. Indent the first line of the paragraph, just as we often do in our own writing system.
2. Leave an empty line or a line with nothing but some ⸪ in it.
3. Make the first tengwa in the first line of the paragraph a big, fancy, gorgeous tengwa with the telcor doubled. This is best suited for formal documents.
4. Use a paragraph ender after the paragraph's last sentence. If that sentence ends with a period, the paragraph ender just replaces it. If it ends with something else, then there is a space and a paragraph ender (usually the :: one).

For the end of the very last paragraph of the document, use this:

∶⁓ text ender

Alphabetic Tengwar Quick Reference Sheet

A		Nasal Tehta	
B		O	
Hard C/K		P	
Soft C		PH	
CH		QU/KW	
Fricative CH		R	
CH said K		S	
D		SH	
E		T	
Silent E		Voiced TH	
F		Voiceless TH	
G		TH said T	
GH		U	
GH said G		V	
H		W	
I		-W	
J		WH	
K/Hard C		X	
L		Consonant Y	
M		Vowel Y	
N		Z	
NG (silent G)		ZH	
NG (heard G)		Tengwa Doubler	

Practice Writing

I organized these exercises by their tyeller, and the tengwar that we don't need have been excluded. Once you've practiced a tyellë, you will learn a vowel tehta so you can start writing words right away.

Tyellë 1: Voiceless Stops

Tinco, used for **T** as in "**t**op, li**tt**le, be**t**."

Parma, used for **P** as in "**p**op, a**pp**le."

Calma, used for **CH** as in "**ch**urch, wat**ch**er."

Quessë, used for **C/K** as in "**c**at, **k**it, ba**ck**." Only use for the hard C pronounced like a K.

Vowel Carriers and Vowel A

Vowel carriers are only used when there is no tengwa following the vowel to put it on.

Telco, used to carry vowels that have no tengwar following them.

Ára, used as an optional alternate to Telco, to carry vowels at the ends of words.

A-tehta, used for **A** as in "<u>a</u>te, br<u>a</u>t, f<u>a</u>ther."

Exercise 1

Write the following words with the Latin alphabet, then practice writing them in tengwar.

1. ᴀpᴀ_____
2. pᴀpᴀ_____
3. ᴀpᴀ_____
4. pᴀpᴀ_____
5. ᴀpᴀ_____
6. ᴀpᴀ_____
7. ᴀpᴀ_____
8. pᴀ_____
9. pᴀpᴀ_____
10. pᴀpᴀ_____
11. ᴀpᴀᴄ_____
12. pᴀpᴀᴄ_____

Tyellë 2: Voiced Stops and Vowel E

Ando, used for **D** as in "**d**ot, ri**dd**le, be**d**."

Umbar, used for **B** as in "**B**o**b**, pe**bb**le."

Anga, used for **J** as in "**j**udge, ob**j**ect."

Ungwë, used for **G** as in "**g**a**g**, e**dg**e, **g**enre."

E-tehta, used for **E** as in "**e**v**e**r." Don't use for a silent E.

Exercise 2

Write the following words with the Latin alphabet, then copy them.

1. ccjṗ _____
2. ꝑꝑj̈ _____
3. ꝑj́ _____
4. ꝑꝑṗ _____
5. ꝑꝑ́ꝑ _____
6. ⱷjṗ _____
7. ꝑṗ _____
8. ⱷjⱷj̈ _____
9. ccjṗ _____
10. ꝑꝑṗ _____
11. ꝑṗq _____
12. cjṗ _____

Tyellë 3: Voiceless Fricatives and Vowel I

Thúlë, used for **TH** as in "**th**ought, no**th**ing, ba**th**." This is for the voiceless TH only.

Formen, used for **F** as in "**f**ox, ra**ff**le, o**ff**."

Harma, used for **SH** as in "**sh**out, wa**sh**," the French-derived **CH** as in "**ch**ampagne, ma**ch**ine," and **S** pronounced like an SH as in "**s**ugar."

Hwesta, used for **CH** as in "lo**ch**." Only use for the fricative CH.

I-tehta, used for **I** as in "evil, bike, machine."

Exercise 3

Write the following words with the Latin alphabet, then copy them.

1. ả̃l_____
2. clṕ̣ə_____
3. hṗ̣q_____
4. pəlḃ_____
5. bṗ̣_____
6. ḃp_____
7. ḃ_____
8. pəả̃l_____
9. clṗ_____
10. qả̃l_____
11. bḃb_____
12. bǧ̇p_____

17

Extended Voiceless Tengwar and Silent E

Extended Thúlë/Tinco, used for **TH** as in "**Th**omas, **Th**ames." This is for the TH pronounced as a T.

Extended Formen/Parma, used for **PH** as in "**ph**one, gra**ph**."

Extended Harma, used for **SH** as in "**sh**out, wa**sh**," the French-derived **CH** as in "**ch**ampagne, ma**ch**ine," and **S** pronounced like an SH as in "**s**ugar." It is interchangeable with Harma.

Extended Hwesta/Quessë, used for **CH** as in "**Ch**ristmas, Mi**ch**ael." Only use for the CH pronounced like a K.

Silent E-tehta, used for **E** as in "wrot**e**, kit**e**, sinc**e**." It goes on the tengwa before it.

Exercise 4

Write the following words with the Latin alphabet, then copy them.

1. ajsö _____
2. þß _____
3. þßí _____
4. ßþö _____
5. þßïï _____
6. þi _____
7. ąí _____
8. ą _____
9. aḃ _____
10. ḃa _____
11. aß _____
12. aąṫí _____

Tyellë 4: Voiced Fricatives and Vowel O

Anto, used for **TH** as in "**th**at, mo**th**er, ba**the**." Only use for the voiced TH.

Ampa, used for **V** as in "**v**ery, i**v**ory, ga**ve**."

Anca, used for **S/Z** as in "trea**s**ure, a**z**ure."

Unquë, used for **GH** as in "dau**gh**ter, cou**gh**, thou**gh**."

O-tehta, used for **O** as in "b**o**t, p**o**pe, **o**pen."

Exercise 5

Write the following words with the Latin alphabet, then copy them.

1. ????
2. ????
3. ????
4. ????
5. ????
6. ????
7. ????
8. ????
9. ????
10. ????
11. ????
12. ????

Extended Voiced Tengwar

Extended Anto, used as the shorthand of the word "the."

Extended Ampa, used as the shorthand of the word "of."

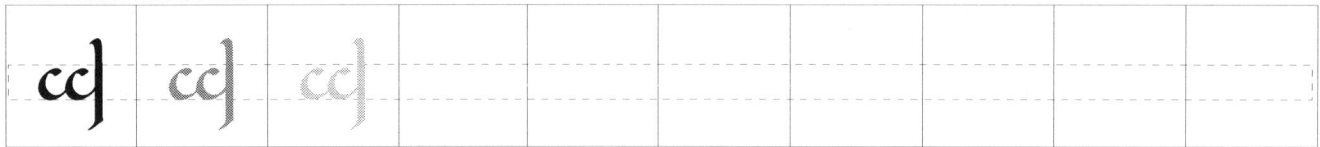

Extended Anca, used for **S/Z** as in "trea**s**ure, a**z**ure." This isn't attested, but it's hypothetically an alternate to Anca.

Extended Unquë/Ungwë, used for **GH** pronounced like a G as in "**gh**ost."

Exercise 6

Write the following words with the Latin alphabet, then copy them.

1. cl̈ḧ_____
2. cl̈ǧ_____
3. cl̈p̂_____
4. hg̈_____
5. hb̂p_____
6. cǰp̂ſ_____
7. œǰp̈_____
8. ȷœ_____
9. ȷœ_____
10. ccp̋_____
11. œœp̈_____
12. c̈c̈ȷï_____

Tyellë 5: Nasals and Vowel U

Númen, used for **N** as in "**n**ope, a**n**yone, ma**n**."

Malta, used for **M** as in "**m**o**m**, **m**u**mm**y."

Ñwalmë, used for **NG** as in "si**ng**." Only for the NG with an inaudible G, like the NG at the ends of words. If you want an NG where the G is heard as in "fi**ng**er," go to page 36.

U-tehta, used for **U** as in "b**u**t, **u**nder, Z**u**l**u**."

Exercise 7

Write the following words with the Latin alphabet, then copy them.

1. ná _____
2. nán _____
3. nó _____
4. né _____
5. ca _____
6. sca _____
7. rca _____
8. so _____
9. nás _____
10. no _____
11. o _____
12. no _____

Tyellë 6: Approximants and Vowel Y

Órë, used for **R** as in "bake**r**, a**r**ching." Rómen is also used for R; see page 28.

Vala, used for **W** as in "**w**ow, a**w**esome." Also used for digraphs that end in U or W as in "ta**u**ght, bo**w**l," which is described on page 40.

Anna, used for **Y** as in "**y**ellow, law**y**er." This is for the consonant Y only. This tengwa is also used for digraphs that end in Y or I as in "ba**y**, co**i**n," which is described on page 38.

Y-tehta, used for **Y** as in "t**y**pical, sc**y**the." Not for the consonant Y. When it occurs at the ends of words, it's usually written with Ára, as in "b**y**, happ**y**."

Exercise 8

Write the following words with the Latin alphabet, then copy them.

1. ᴇʟꜰ _____
2. ɪ _____
3. ʜɪꜱ _____
4. ᴛᴏ _____
5. ꜱɪꜱ _____
6. ᴛʜɪꜱ _____
7. ꜱʜᴏꜱ _____
8. ɪꜰᴏꜱ _____
9. ᴇꜰᴏ _____
10. ꜱᴏᴛᴏꜰ _____
11. ᴏꜰᴇꜱ _____
12. ᴏᴛᴀᴇʟ _____

Tyellë 7: More Approximants and Double Vowels AA

Rómen, used for **R** as in "**r**un, sc**r**ibe." Órë is also used for R. People like using them based on their Quenya usage: Rómen when the following letter is a vowel, and Órë the rest of the time. Silent E isn't counted as a vowel, as in "acr**e**."

If you speak a dialect that drops R's, you may want to use Rómen and Órë slightly differently. You can use Órë for dropped R's, and Rómen for retained R's.

Lambë, used for **L** as in "**l**awn, **l**ily, va**ll**ey, app**l**e." Marks that normally go under a tengwa like the silent E go inside its lúva. The example below features a silent E.

Double A, used for **AA** as in "**aa**rdvark." The second A is put on the following tengwa, if there is one. This is how double vowels are often written.

Exercise 9

Write the following words with the Latin alphabet, then copy them.

1. yp̂ _____
2. pn̆ _____
3. ͼẗdp _____
4. pyẗdp _____
5. pͼ _____
6. pp̊ͼ _____
7. ïẙm̂ _____
8. qċdïͼ _____
9. ym̊ _____
10. nyp̂ _____
11. þp̂ḋyp̂ _____
12. yͼþ _____

29

Tyellë 8: S and Z and Double Vowels EE

Silmë, used for **S** as in "**s**top, **s**i**s**ter, lo**ss**." Some fonts don't combine Silmë with tehtar over it gracefully, so you can use Silmë Nuquerna as an alternate.

Silmë Nuquerna, used for **C** pronounced like an S or SH as in "**c**elery, spe**c**ial, mi**c**e." It's also an alternate for Silmë when you can't fit tehtar over Silmë. The font I used[3] in this book doesn't have this problem.

Ázë, used for **Z/S** as in "**z**oo, wi**s**e." Use for an S that sounds like a Z. This tengwa is better for tehtar underneath it than over it. For tehtar over it, use Ázë Nuquerna.

Ázë Nuquerna, used for **Z/S** as in "topa**z**, i**s**." Use for an S that sounds like a Z. This tengwa is better for tehtar over it than underneath it. For tehtar under it, use Ázë.

Double E, used for **EE** as in "**ee**rie, r**ee**d, Ren**ée**." Can be written separately or by doubling it over the tengwa. I'm using Úrë to stand in for the tengwa here.

---

3 Tengwar Telcontar, my all-time favorite. Isn't it beautiful?

Exercise 10

Write the following words with the Latin alphabet, then copy them.

1. mípa _____
2. gur _____
3. lost _____
4. peda _____
5. laa _____
6. estel _____
7. luthe _____
8. gwain _____
9. gurpit _____
10. gwad _____
11. eth _____
12. leppa _____

Tyellë 9: H and WH and Double Vowels OO and UU

Hyarmen, used for **H** as in "**h**op, key**h**ole." Don't use for digraphs like WH, CH, SH, TH, etc.

Hwesta Sindarinwa, used for **WH** as in "**wh**at." This symbol is written in three different ways.

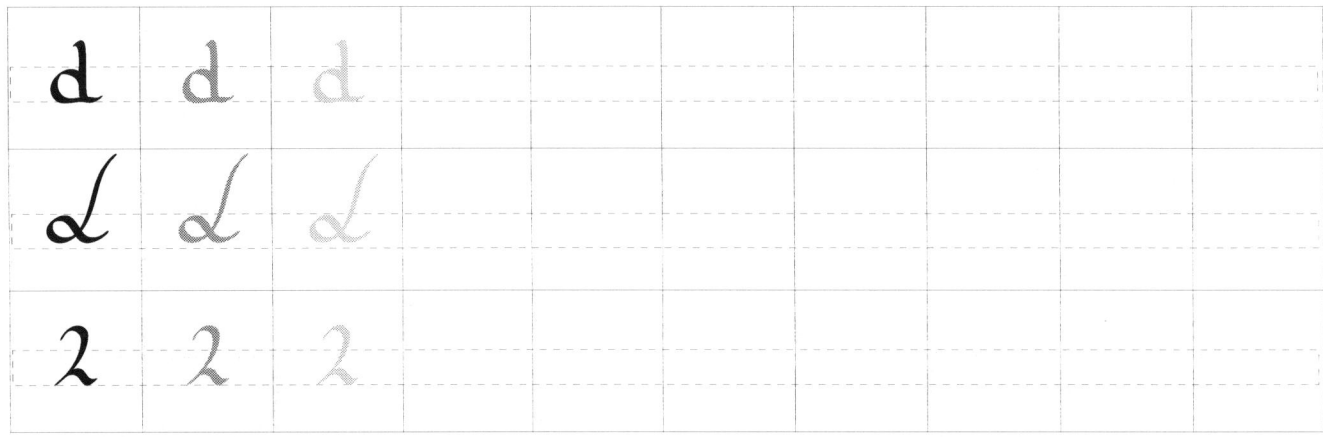

Double O, used for **OO** as in "b**oo**t." Can be written separately or by doubling it over the tengwa. I'm using Úrë to stand in for the tengwa here.

Double U, used for **UU** as in "contin**uu**m." Written separately because these are said separately.

Exercise 11

Write the following words with the Latin alphabet, then copy them.

1. dm̌ _____
2. pÿiλ _____
3. pypm̌ _____
4. λŏpŷj _____
5. mícďh _____
6. λḣ _____
7. díŧ _____
8. pq̃ _____
9. bŧj _____
10. ŏẏλ _____
11. bq̃jm̌ _____
12. cpλ _____

Digraphs

A digraph is two letters side by side, used as a single unit. In tengwar, vowel digraphs are written two ways: with the first vowel as a tehta and the second as a tengwa, or with both vowels as tehtar. Consonant digraphs are a combination of a tengwa and a tehta. The most common digraphs are included.

-A Digraphs and Double Consonants

Ossë, used for digraphs that end in A, as in "b**ea**t, b**oa**t." This digraph is often written with two vowel-tehtar, more than other vowel digraphs, so I've listed those versions as well.

Consonant Doubler Tehta, used to double any consonant tengwa, as in "ba**ck**, mu**mm**y, gri**zz**ly, rea**ll**y, le**ss**, a**rr**ow, ba**tch**." Note its placement and length with different sorts of tengwar.

- CK counts as a double consonant.
- TCH can be written either T-CH or as a doubled CH.
- NN and MM can also be written with the Nasal-tehta, though which you choose should be kept consistent throughout the text.

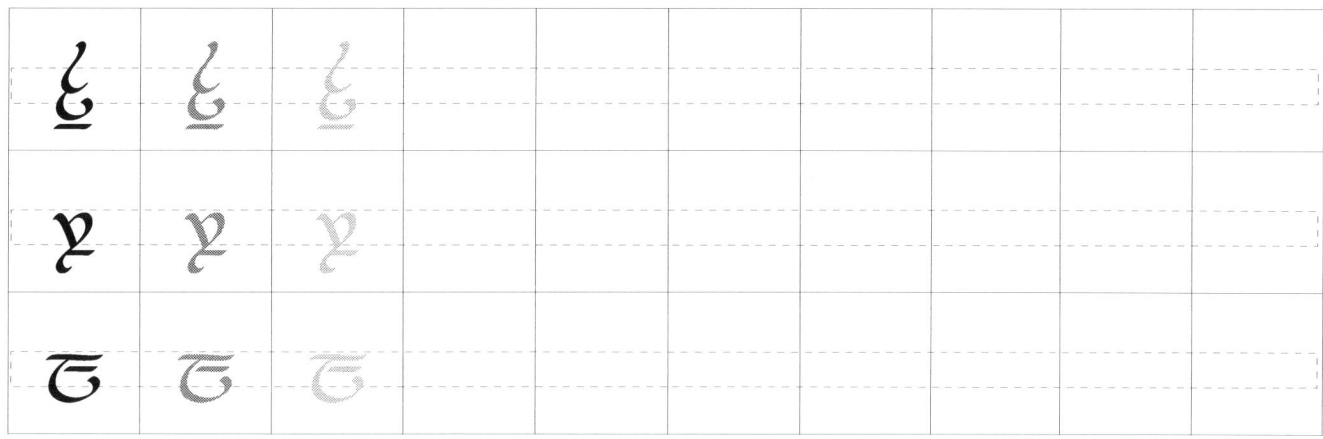

Exercise 12

The exercises are getting a little more difficult. Now you will have to transcribe short phrases.

Write the following phrases with the Latin alphabet, then copy them in tengwar.

1. _____
2. _____
3. _____
4. _____
5. _____
6. _____
7. _____
8. _____
9. _____
10. _____
11. _____
12. _____

-E Digraphs and Nasals + Stops

Yanta, used in digraphs that end in E, as in "p**ie**ce, Mich**ae**l, d**ye**, sh**oe**." These are sometimes also written as two separate vowels, like with the -A digraphs above.

Nasal-tehta, used to add a nasal consonant before a tengwa from the 1st, 2nd, or 5th tyeller. It becomes an **M** proceeding a tengwa from the Parmatéma as in "a**m**p, mu**m**my, a**m**ber." It becomes an **N** proceeding the other tengwar, as in "a**n**t, u**n**der, be**n**ch, ora**n**ge, tha**n**k, a**n**ger, A**n**ne."

- Don't use this when the G is silent in NG. Use Ñwalmë instead.
- NN and MM can also be written with the consonant doubler tehta, though which you choose should be kept consistent throughout the text.

Note how it matches the length of the tengwa it is attached to.

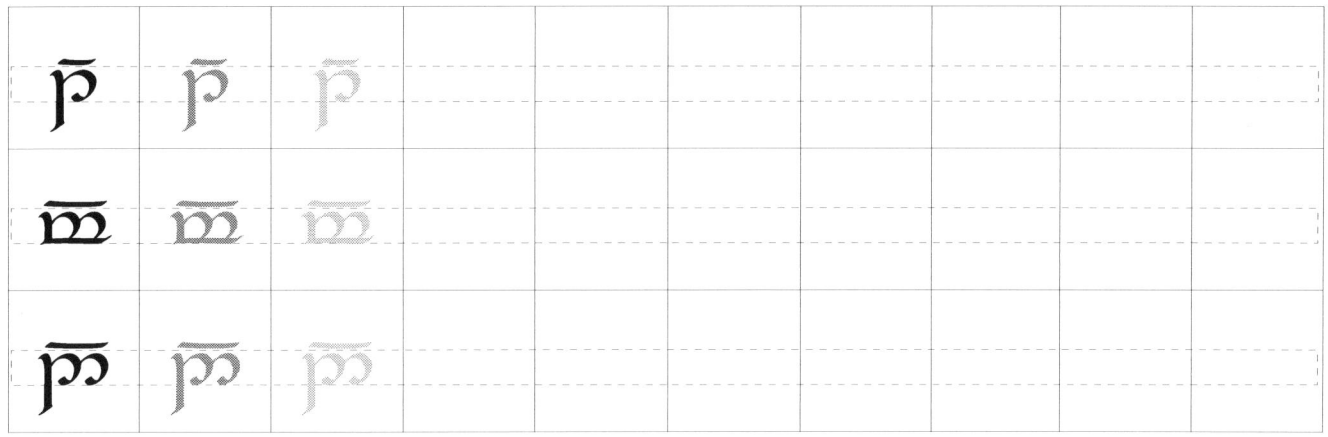

Exercise 13

Write the following phrases with the Latin alphabet, then copy them.

1. _____
2. _____
3. _____
4. _____
5. _____
6. _____
7. _____
8. _____
9. _____
10. _____
11. _____
12. _____

-I/Y Digraphs and the W-Tehta

Anna, used for digraphs that end in Y or I, as in "b**ai**t, r**ay**, **ei**ght, gr**ey**, b**oy**, m**oi**st, r**ui**n"

W-tehta, used for **W** when it follows a tengwa, as in "t**w**o, q**u**een, G**w**en." QU is written KW. Note that it lengthens to match the width of the tengwa it is attached to.

When combined with other tehtar, the order from top to bottom is: vowel-tehta on top, W-tehta, then the Nasal-tehta, as in the word "tengwar" in the title of the book. See also page 7.

Exercise 14

Write the following phrases with the Latin alphabet, then copy them.

1. ꜩꜩ ꜩꜩ _____
2. ꜩꜩꜩꜩ ꜩꜩꜩꜩ _____
3. ꜩꜩ ꜩꜩ ꜩꜩ ꜩꜩꜩ _____
4. ꜩꜩꜩ ꜩꜩ ꜩꜩꜩ _____
5. ꜩꜩ ꜩꜩꜩ ꜩꜩ ꜩꜩꜩꜩ _____
6. ꜩꜩ ꜩ ꜩꜩꜩ _____
7. ꜩꜩꜩ ꜩ ꜩ ꜩꜩꜩ _____
8. ꜩꜩ ꜩꜩꜩ _____
9. ꜩꜩꜩ ꜩꜩ ꜩ ꜩꜩꜩꜩ _____
10. ꜩꜩꜩꜩ ꜩꜩꜩ _____
11. ꜩꜩ ꜩꜩ ꜩꜩꜩꜩ _____
12. ꜩꜩꜩ ꜩꜩꜩ _____

39

-U/W Digraphs and the S-Tehta

Vala, used for digraphs that end in U or W, as in "y**ou**, **ow**l, **aw**e, l**au**gh, **Eu**rope, f**ew**."

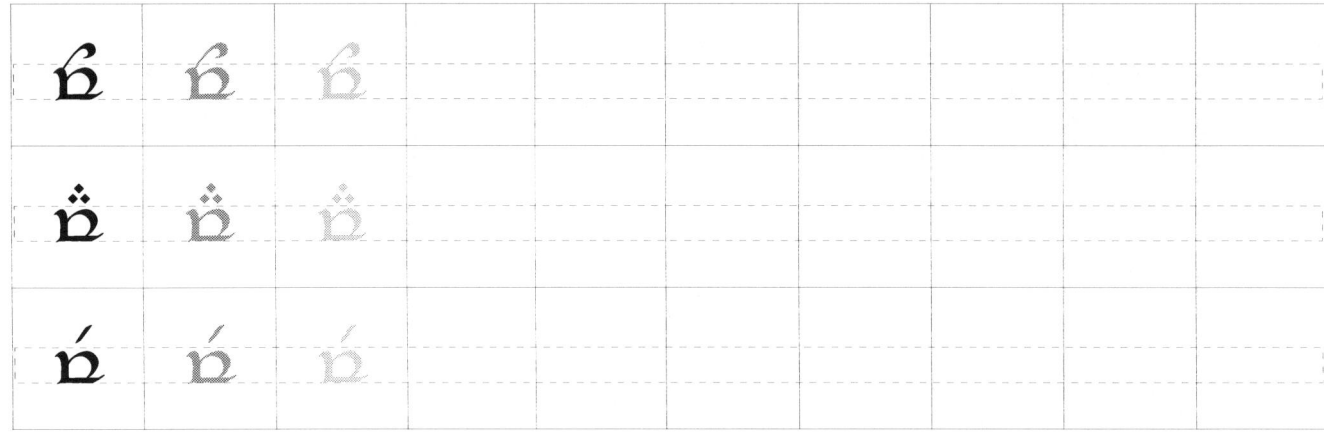

Sa-rincë, used in combination with Quessë for **X** as in "Re**x**, **x**ylophone."

Spacing Sa-rincë, used for **S** when it is suffixed onto a word ending with a tengwa as in "fit**s**, mom**s**, ring**s**, call**s**." This S can be pronounced like an S or Z. Note where it attaches to the telcor on left-facing lúvar. It has a fancy alternate version that makes a loop.

If the suffix is "-es" instead of "-s", as in "bush**es**, mass**es**, tax**es**" then you'd add an E-tehta over it, because the Spacing Sa-rincë can take vowel-tehtar! It's demonstrated on the Quessë and Telco.

Exercise 15

Write the following phrases with the Latin alphabet, then copy them.

1. _____
2. _____
3. _____
4. _____
5. _____
6. _____
7. _____
8. _____
9. _____
10. _____
11. _____
12. _____

Christopher's Numbers

Numbers are written in reverse order from how we do it, so the number "400" would be written "004." Also, numbers like "first, third, sixth" are spelled out. There is no abbreviation for them.

Tolkien had multiple versions of his numerals. This set was described by his son, Christopher Tolkien, and it is most widely used by fans because we've known about it the longest.

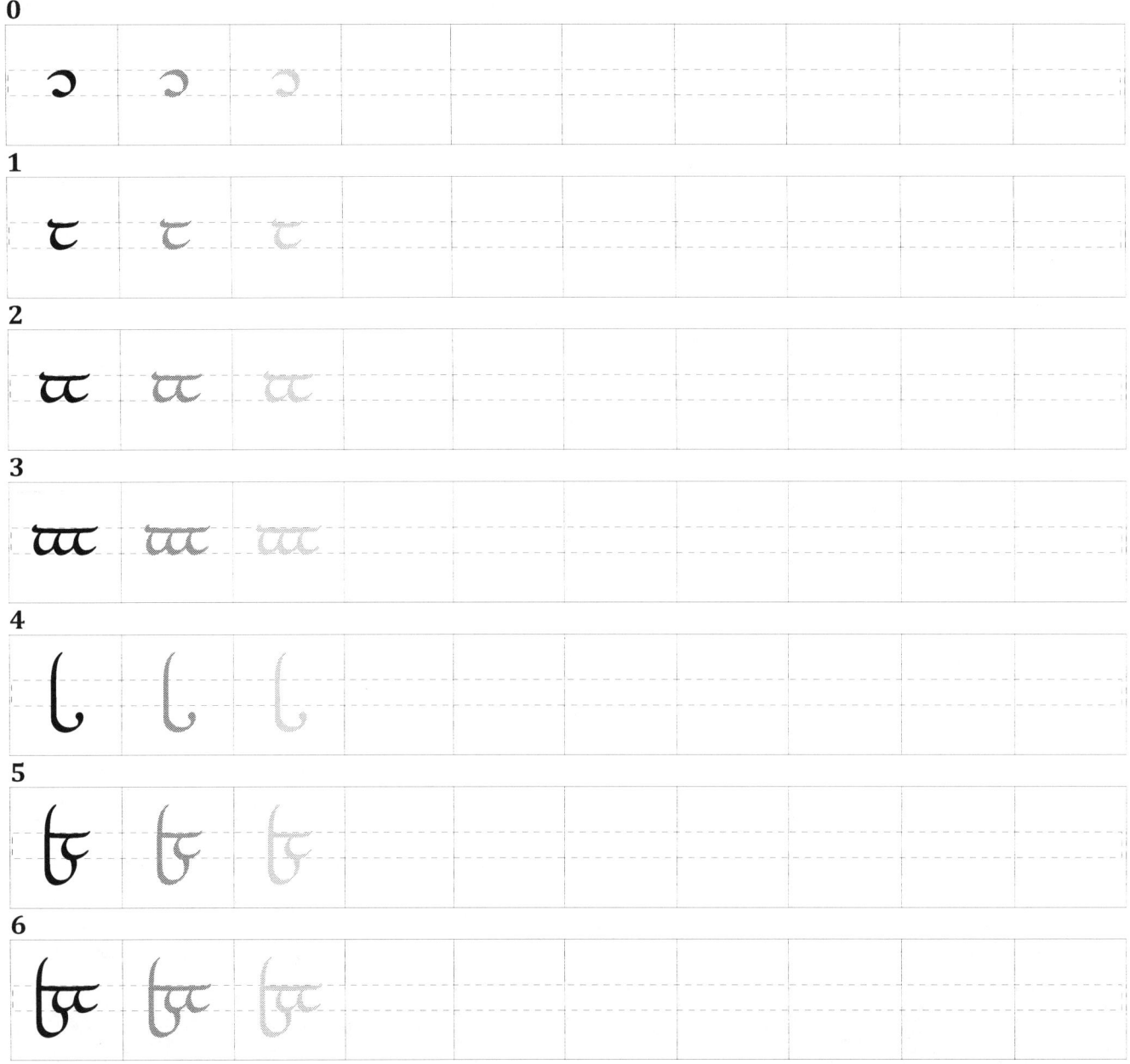

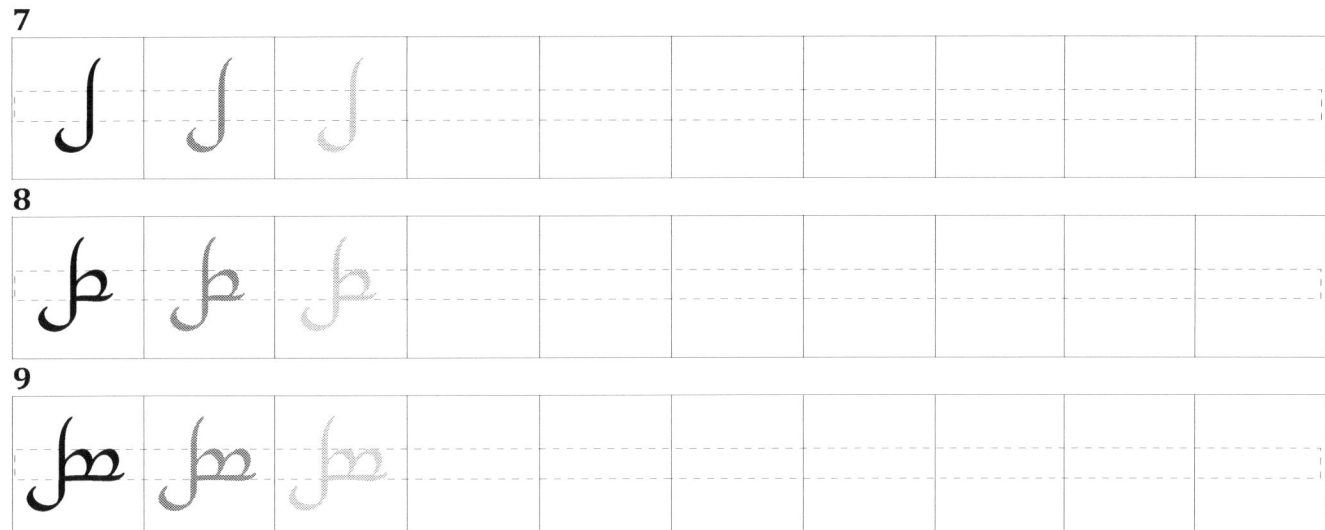

Exercise 16

Write the following numbers with the Arabic numerals, then copy them.

1. ݂ݎݕݐݏݐ_____
2. ݂ݐݕݐ_____
3. ݂ݎݏ ݂ݎݏ_____
4. ݏݏݏݏݏݏݐ_____
5. ݐ ݙݐ_____
6. ݐݙݐݐ_____
7. ݂ݎݕݙ_____
8. ݐݙݐ ݂ݐݙݐ_____
9. ݐ ݂ݐݙݐ ݂ݎݐ_____
10. ݂ݎݐ ݙ_____
11. ݂ݎ ݙ_____
12. ݏ ݂ݐݙ_____

43

Tolkien's Numbers

Tolkien had multiple versions of his numerals. The numbers aren't reversed in this version.

0 - Úrë

1 can be written with a Telco or an Ára.

2 - Tinco

3 - Ando

4 - Vala

5 - Ázë

6 - Silmë

7 - Calma

8 - Anga

9 - Rómen

Exercise 17

Write the following numbers with the Arabic numerals, then copy them.

1. þɔi
2. ɴiɜʏ
3. þʎɜ
4. þɔɜccʏɕʏþɔ
5. þþɔcɕ
6. ɴ
7. ʎþʎ
8. ɴþɔþɔ
9. cɕþɔ
10. þɕʏɜ
11. ɜo
12. þcɕ

Shorthand Words

Abbreviations of common words, similar to symbols we use like @, $, %, &, w/o, and #.

"The" This is occasionally written with a dot under it to mark it as an abbreviation. Use whichever you prefer.

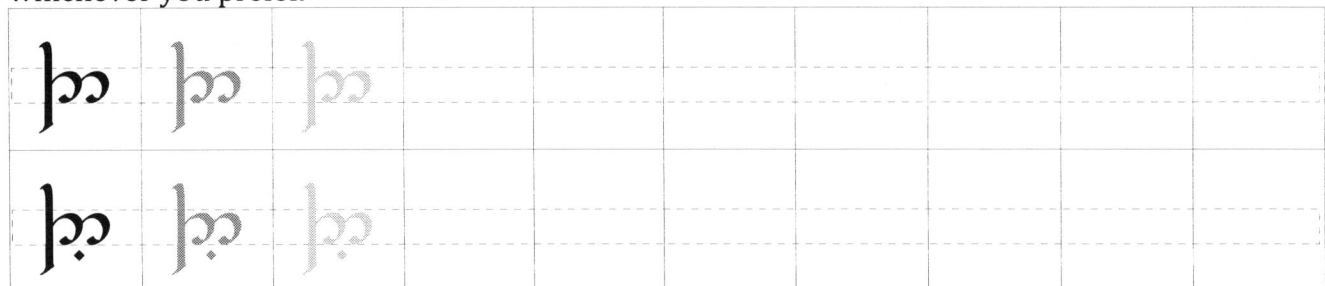

"Of"

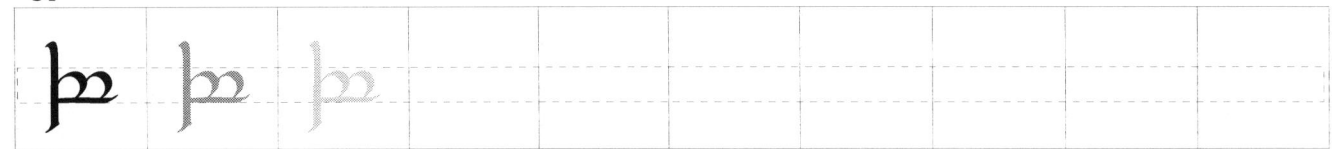

"Of the"

"And" This is occasionally written with a dot under it to mark it as an abbreviation. Use whichever you prefer.

Punctuation Marks

Tengwar punctuation is a little different from punctuation in the Latin alphabet. There isn't a one-to-one equivalence. There are no apostrophes, like in "isn't" or "o'clock," and no hyphens for compound-words. Also, tengwar punctuation marks require a space on either side of them unless they are at the beginning or end of a line.

Tolkien used Latin punctuation instead in some texts, but he never mixed them.

Dots

Dots indicate pauses. The more dots, the stronger the pause and more end-like it is.

One Dot, a short pause. It usually used as an equivalent for a comma or semicolon.

•	•	•							

Two Dots, a regular pause. It's usually used as a period or a semicolon. It has an alternate short form, where one just makes the lower dot.

:	:	:							

•	•	•							

Three Dots, a strong pause. It's usually used as period or to mark the end of a paragraph. I like to use it as an ellipsis as well. It has two different ways it can be written interchangeably.

∴	∴	∴							

⋮	⋮	⋮							

Four Dots, a very strong pause. It's used for the ends of paragraphs or the ends of texts. Turned up on its end, it's often used as a decorative line break or to mark out/emphasize something.

You can do more dots if you wish.............................. but this is what we have examples of.

Sentences

Parentheses take the place of any other punctuation and have a space on either side of them. They have a variety of forms. You'll use the same symbol to mark the beginning and the end. These forms aren't mixed and should be kept consistent throughout a document.

One of the forms the parentheses can take looks a lot like quotation marks. The upper parenthesis marks the beginning and the lower parenthesis marks the end. These are also used to mark when a word is in a different mode or language, letting the reader they need to reorient themselves for the differing use of the tengwar.

Hyphen, used when a word is split because it doesn't fit on a line. This mark isn't mandatory, and it's just as acceptable to break apart the word at the end of the line without marking it at all.

48

Exclamation Point, replaces a period at the end of a sentence.

Question Mark, replaces a period at the end of a sentence.

Paragraphs, Verses, and Texts

These are started in a variety of ways and should be kept consistent within a text.

- **Indents** are used to mark the beginnings of paragraphs, much like how they are in Latin texts. It's more common in plain prose without any decoration.
- **An Empty Line** between paragraphs is another way to separate them. We don't see this as often because Tolkien was likely trying to save space on a page, but it is a viable option.

    Sometimes there are ⸫ in the line, so there is something decorative in the line.
- **A Big, Fancy Tengwa** at the beginning of a line marks the start of a paragraph. If the tengwa has a telco, then the telco is often turned into a double-bar. These can get very ornate, and if you are a calligrapher, this is where you let your skill shine. This style of paragraph marking is used for formal documents and verse.

The paragraph enders are the 3-dot or 4-dot marks. If the paragraph ends with a period, the period is usually replaced with the paragraph ender. If the paragraph ends with a parenthesis, question mark, or exclamation point, then follow it with a little space and the 4-dot paragraph ender.

When you end the text, you can finish it with a 4-dot mark or a text ender.

Text Ending Mark – this one just replaces the period at the end of the text. If it ends in one of the non-dot marks, you can just add the tilde to the existing mark. In more formal documents, you can turn this into a pretty drawing of a branch or flower.

Let's Put it All Together!

First, try to read this section of Lord Alfred Tennyson's poem *The Lady of Shallot*. The answers are at the end of the book.

Now let's transliterate the next verse of the poem.

> Willows whiten, aspens shiver.
> The sunbeam showers break and quiver
> In the stream that runneth ever
> By the island in the river
> Flowing down to Camelot.
> Four gray walls, and four gray towers
> Overlook a space of flowers,
> And the silent isle imbowers
> The Lady of Shalott.

"My dearest Lucy,—

Forgive my long delay in writing, but I have been simply overwhelmed with work. The life of an assistant schoolmistress is sometimes trying. I am longing to be with you, and by the sea, where we can talk together freely and build our castles in the air. I have been working very hard lately, because I want to keep up with Jonathan's studies, and I have been practising shorthand very assiduously. When we are married I shall be able to be useful to Jonathan, and if I can stenograph well enough I can take down what he wants to say in this way and write it out for him on the typewriter, at which also I am practising very hard.

Transliterate the second half of the letter into tengwar.

I do not suppose there will be much of interest to other people, but it is not intended for them. I may show it to Jonathan some day if there is in it anything worth sharing, but it is really an exercise book. I shall try to do what I see lady journalists do, interviewing and writing descriptions and trying to remember conversations. I am told that, with a little practice, one can remember all that goes on or that one hears said during a day.

However, we shall see. I will tell you of my little plans when we meet. I have just had a few hurried lines from Jonathan from Transylvania. He is well, and will be returning in about a week. I am longing to hear all his news. It must be nice to see strange countries. I wonder if we, I mean Jonathan and I, shall ever see them together. There is the ten o'clock bell ringing. Goodbye.

Your loving Mina

Tell me all the news when you write. You have not told me anything for a long time. I hear rumours, and especially of a tall, handsome, curly-haired man.

Answer Key

Exercise 1
1. cat
2. papa
3. chat
4. tap
5. cap
6. chap
7. act
8. at
9. pat
10. pap
11. catch
12. patch

Exercise 2
1. jet
2. beta
3. be
4. dad
5. debt
6. get
7. tab
8. gaga
9. jab
10. bad
11. batch
12. chad

Exercise 3
1. ash
2. shed
3. thatch
4. bath
5. fat
6. aft
7. if
8. Bach
9. ship
10. cash
11. fifth
12. fact

Exercise 4
1. shade
2. Thoth
3. photo
4. aphid
5. phobia
6. phi
7. echo
8. ache
9. chef
10. fish
11. shop
12. Chicago

Exercise 5
1. that
2. both
3. fight
4. video
5. vapid
6. thigh
7. bathe
8. tithe
9. diva
10. tight
11. vet
12. Asia

Exercise 6
1. shave
2. shock
3. shoot
4. thick
5. theft
6. ghetto
7. vacate
8. of
9. the
10. Jeep
11. vivid
12. Asia

Exercise 7
1. an
2. mama
3. on
4. me
5. king
6. baking
7. faking
8. but
9. naming
10. nut
11. up
12. note

Exercise 8
1. yeti
2. or
3. ever
4. war
5. for
6. mother
7. father
8. order
9. yard
10. synonym
11. butcher
12. anonymity

Exercise 9
1. ride
2. pyre
3. light
4. bright
5. tile
6. table
7. Aaron
8. casual
9. ram
10. write
11. photograph
12. Ralph

Exercise 10
1. need
2. cyst
3. song
4. deed
5. see
6. zinger
7. sister
8. celiac
9. celestial
10. cedar
11. zone
12. speed

Exercise 11
1. when
2. pariah
3. probably
4. history
5. measure
6. whiz
7. wheel
8. book
9. fly
10. Sarah
11. vacuum
12. cheetah

Exercise 12
1. dead on arrival
2. all at once
3. tattle tale
4. happily ever after
5. really fun
6. ready or not
7. once upon a time
8. hello
9. approach at will
10. all aboard
11. float along
12. long support beam

Exercise 13
1. do or die
2. mind over matter
3. goodbye
4. science
5. ancient Roman tomb
6. tasty pie crust
7. long antennae
8. lost in faerie
9. stubbed my toe
10. a leaky canoe
11. gentle as a doe
12. friend or foe

Exercise 14
1. take two
2. woefully inadequate
3. the queen of Spain
4. quest for glory
5. the guest of Gwendolyn
6. what a twist
7. tweak it a little
8. twice done
9. dwelling with a nuisance
10. something weird
11. ray of sunshine
12. royal heir

Exercise 15
1. dusk till dawn
2. tail between his legs
3. knickers in a twist
4. cat got your tongue
5. one thousand miles
6. phenomenal cosmic power
7. it gets louder
8. what's your counter attack
9. claw-like fingers
10. I could do it
11. because of this
12. eyes narrow into slits

Exercise 16
1. 2019
2. 26
3. 99
4. 1 000 000
5. 241
6. 32
7. 467
8. 2531
9. 1861
10. 428
11. 47
12. 460

Exercise 17
1. 31
2. 4159
3. 265
4. 3589793
5. 238
6. 4
7. 626
8. 433
9. 83
10. 2795
11. 50
12. 28

Part 1

On either side the river lie
Long fields of barley and of rye,
That clothe the wold and meet the sky,
And through the field the road runs by
To many-towered Camelot,
The yellow-leaved waterlily
The green-sheathed daffodilly
Tremble in the water chilly
Round about Shalott.

Part 2

[Tengwar script text]

Part 3

My dearest Lucy

Forgive my long delay in writing, but I have been simply overwhelmed with work. The life of an assistant schoolmistress is sometimes trying. I am longing to be with you, and by the sea, where we can talk together freely and build our castles in the air. I have been working very hard lately, because I want to keep up with Jonathan's studies, and I have been practicing shorthand very assiduously. When we are married I shall be able to be useful to Jonathan, and if I can stenograph well enough I can take down what he wants to say in this way and write it out for him on the typewriter, at which also I am practicing very hard.

He and I sometimes write letters in shorthand, and he is keeping a stenographic journal of his travels abroad. When I am with you I shall keep a diary in the same way. I don't mean one of those two pages to the week with Sunday squeezed in a corner diaries, but a sort of journal which I can write in whenever I feel inclined.

Part 4

Made in the USA
Coppell, TX
20 October 2023

23118938R00033